The Amazing Adventures of Misty Rose – Coming Home!

By Carol Ann Young

Illustrated by Shara Nunez

Copyright © 2013 Carol Ann Young

All rights reserved.

ISBN: 0615801803
ISBN-13: 978-0615801803

DEDICATION

This book is dedicated to my darling grand daughter, Jaimee.
Darling Jaimee, you are the beat of my heart. I love you.

Ninny

ACKNOWLEDGMENTS

This is to acknowledge the work of Cheryl Bond, as friend, editor and advisor. Thanks so much, you are awesome.

Also to Shara Nunez, for bringing my story to life. Thank you, from both Misty Rose and me. Your drawings are amazing!

My name is Misty Rose. I am a puppy. My name, when I was born, was Noelle. I guess they gave me that name because I was born on December 23.

I have two brothers and two sisters.
It was fun playing with my family.
We always had a good time.

One day, we had a visitor who came and held me in her arms. She said she was my new Mommy. I was so scared.

She took me to live with her. After a long ride, we arrived in my new home.

It was so lonely without my family. I cried myself to sleep that night. It was so scary!

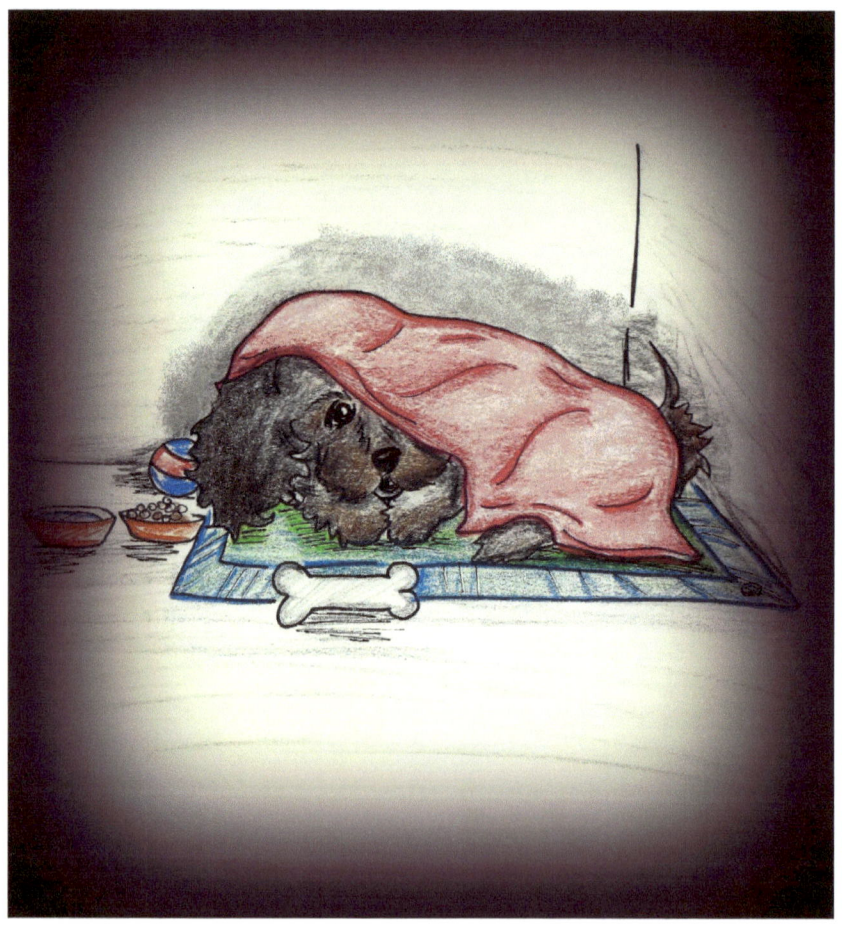

When I woke up, my new Mommy was there. There was also a nice little girl named Jaimee, who played with me.

My new Mommy would hold me when I got scared of something new that I didn't understand.

It was fun running in the backyard with her. Jaimee couldn't catch me. She would hug me and hold me. She made me feel so good.

I chased a ball…

The Amazing Adventures of Misty Rose

I chased a squirrel…

I chased some leaves. It was fun, and I wasn't as scared as I was yesterday.

I still missed my brothers and sisters. But, Jaimee would hold me and it was nice. She would hug away my being scared.

At night, Mommy would tuck me in bed with my favorite toy…Mr. Dolphin.

I began to realize that if something scared me, I could go to Mommy. She would explain away my being scared. I loved it when Mommy would kiss away my worries.

Mommy made sure I was safe. That is what families are for; to make sure you are safe.

Mommy made sure she taught me what was safe and what wasn't. This way, I did not have to be scared all the time.

I loved running around my yard! It had a fence, so I couldn't play with all the dogs walking by…but Mommy said it would keep me safe.

Mommy's friends would bring their dogs over so we could all play. I have a bunch of new friends and we have a lot of fun!

I realize now, that I am a "big girl". When I am scared, I have my Mommy and people who love me to keep me safe. No one would let me do something that would hurt me. You have to be brave, and sometimes you have to try new things to have special adventures. Sometimes you like them, and sometimes you don't. However, I wouldn't know if I didn't try new things and learn to be brave.

THE END

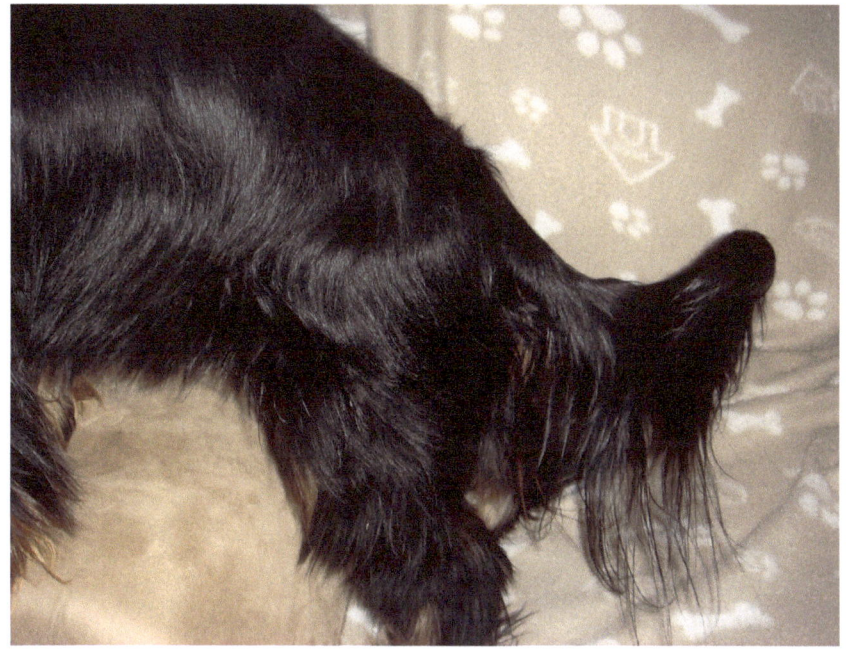

Carol Ann Young

ABOUT THE AUTHOR

Carol Ann Young lives in Winter Springs, Fl., with her dog Misty Rose. This is her first book; written especially for her Grand daughter, Jaimee. Her objective in writing this book was to teach small children there are things that might make them scared; but there will always be people who love them and will keep them safe.

www.ingramcontent.com/pod-product-compliance
Lightning Source LLC
Chambersburg PA
CBHW041745040426
42444CB00001B/33